URBAN LEGENDS • DON'T READ ALONE!

# STONEHENGE

This series features unsolved mysteries, urban legends, and other curious stories. Each creepy, shocking, or befuddling book focuses on what people believe and hear. True or not? That's for you to decide!

45th Parallel Press

Published in the United States of America by Cherry Lake Publishing
Ann Arbor, Michigan
www.cherrylakepublishing.com

Author: Virginia Loh-Hagan
Reading Adviser: Marla Conn MS, Ed., Literacy specialist, Read-Ability, Inc.
Book Designer: Felicia Macheske

Photo Credits: © Photo Credits: © Filip Fuxa/Shutterstock.com, cover; © SOMMAI/Shutterstock.com, cover; © shootmybusiness/Shutterstock.com, 5; © 1000 Words/Shutterstock.com, 7; © Komsan Sangaroon/ Shutterstock.com, 8; © Dutourdumonde Photography/Shutterstock.com, 11; © Christopher Watkins/ Shutterstock.com, 13; © Vadim Petrakov/Shutterstock.com, 14; © Ksenia Konakova/Shutterstock.com, 17; © SherSS/Shutterstock.com, 18; © Zoran Pavlovikj/Shutterstock.com, 21; © Pius Lee/Shutterstock.com, 24; © Polina Nefidova/Shutterstock.com, 27; © lexar001/Shutterstock.com, 29

Graphic Elements Throughout: © iofoto/Shutterstock.com; © COLCU/Shutterstock.com; © spacedrone808/ Shutterstock.com; © rf.vector.stock/Shutterstock.com; © donatas1205/Shutterstock.com; © cluckva/ Shutterstock.com; © Eky Studio/Shutterstock.com



**45th Parallel Press** is an imprint of Cherry Lake Publishing.

Library of Congress Cataloging-in-Publication Data

Names: Loh-Hagan, Virginia, author.
Title: Stonehenge / by Dr. Virginia Loh-Hagan.
Description: Ann Arbor : Cherry Lake Publishing, 2018. | Series: Urban legends: don't read alone! | Includes bibliographical references and index. | Audience: Grades 4-6.
Identifiers: LCCN 2017035949| ISBN 9781534107663 (hardcover) | ISBN 9781534109643 (pdf) | ISBN 9781534108653 (pbk.) | ISBN 9781534120631 (hosted ebook)
Subjects: LCSH: Stonehenge (England)--Juvenile literature.
Classification: LCC DA142 .L83 2018 | DDC 936.2/319--dc23
LC record available at https://lccn.loc.gov/2017035949

Cherry Lake Publishing would like to acknowledge the work of The Partnership for 21st Century Skills. Please visit *www.p21.org* for more information.

Printed in the United States of America
Corporate Graphics

# TABLE OF CONTENTS

# Chapter One

# SCARY STONES

What are some disappearances at Stonehenge? What are some strange things that happened at Stonehenge?

Stonehenge is a **monument** of huge stones. Monuments are structures. They honor something. Stonehenge is located in Wiltshire, England.

Something strange happened in August 1971. A group of **hippies** camped out at Stonehenge. Hippies are free spirits. They don't believe in traditional values.

These hippies pitched tents. They did this in the center of the Stonehenge circle. They spent the night around a campfire. At 2:00 a.m., there was a thunderstorm. Lightning hit the stones. There was a blue light. The hippies screamed. Then, they disappeared. Only burning tent pegs and the campfire were left.

There are several urban legends about Stonehenge.

# CONSIDER THE EVIDENCE

Druids were people in ancient Great Britain and France. They were pagans. Pagans believe in many gods. They worship nature. Many people think the Druids built Stonehenge. They think Stonehenge was part of the Druids' pagan rituals. Rituals are ceremonies. But scientists found that Druids couldn't have built Stonehenge. The scientists did tests. They found that Stonehenge was built before Druids came to be. The Druids formed around the year 300 BCE. Stonehenge was built years before then. Also, Druids did their rituals in the woods or mountains. They wouldn't have used an open field.

There was another disappearance. A man went to Stonehenge. He was talking to a couple. The couple told him they were hundreds of years old. Later, the man turned to question the couple. The couple was gone.

Some people reported seeing a ghost. The ghost is a young boy. The ghost is seen walking among the stones. The nearby town also has a lot of ghost stories.

Visitors take pictures of Stonehenge. They have reported odd things happening to their pictures. They look at their cameras. The pictures got deleted. Or the pictures have weird things in them.

Strange things happen around Stonehenge.

Angels are God's messengers.

In 2014, Toby Elles was visiting friends near Stonehenge. He was on a bus. It was early evening. The sun had just gone down. The clouds lit up. There were beautiful colors in the sky. Elles looked out the window. He said, "I looked up and saw a vivid cloud formation of what looked like an angel above the Stonehenge area." He took pictures of it. He thought the angel meant something.

Elles has seen strange things before. In 2010, he saw Jesus Christ in his frying pan. He said, "I am unsure why religious symbols keep appearing to me. Maybe I'm blessed."

# Chapter Two

# SPECIAL STONES

What is a henge? What does Stonehenge look like? Why is Stonehenge a mystery?

A **henge** is a circle of stones or wooden posts. Stonehenge is a special type of henge. It's a ring of standing stones. It's in an open field. It was built over 5,000 years ago. It's part of a bigger system. There are over 1,000 henges in Europe. Stonehenge is the most popular. More than 800,000 people visit Stonehenge each year.

Stonehenge is made of **megaliths**. Megaliths are single large stones. They're arranged in a circle. "Mega" means great. "Lithos" means stones. England has the most megaliths.

"Henge" is an Old English word. It means hang.

## SPOTLIGHT

# BIOGRAPHY

Christie Willis is an archaeologist. She studies human history. She's an expert on human remains. She's working on her doctorate at University College London's Institute of Archaeology. She's studying Stonehenge. She made a big discovery. Her team found skeletons. The bones were mixed together. Willis sorted through 100 pounds (45 kilograms) of bones. She studied the bones. She studied the ear canals. The bones around the ear canal are strong. They survive fire. Willis used these bones to determine the sex. She identified 14 females and 9 males. Willis also found long bone pins. These pins were used as hairpins.

Stonehenge has about 100 stones. The stones are **upright**. This means they stand straight up. These stones are huge. They're shaped like rectangles. The biggest stones are called **sarsens**. They're 30 feet (9 meters) tall. They're 7 feet (2 m) wide. They weigh 25 tons. The smaller stones are called **bluestones**. They have hints of blue when wet or broken. They weigh 4 tons.

Bluestones are special. They were the first stones at Stonehenge. They're thought to have healing powers. They cure sicknesses. People chipped away at the bluestones. They kept bits. They wanted to heal themselves.

Stonehenge was built with the sun in mind. On special days, it aligns with the sunset and sunrise.

Some people think icebergs carried the stones over.

The stones are not natural to the area. They came from other areas. They were brought from far away. But the stones are too big to be moved. And yet, Stonehenge exists. How did the stones get there? Ancient people moved them without modern tools. The wheel wasn't even invented yet. Some experts think ancient people made a track. They used logs. They rolled the stones on the log tracks. They floated them on logs down a river. Other experts think ancient people made a sled. They used animal fat to grease the road.

Stonehenge is a mystery. The people who built Stonehenge left no written records. No one knows how the rocks got there. No one knows why it was built. But people have many ideas.

Chapter Three

# A STONY PAST

What is the history of Stonehenge? What are the three phases of building?

Ancient people took about 1,500 years to build Stonehenge. It was built in three phases. It was built over a long time. It was built between 3000 BCE and 1600 BCE. It was finished in the **Bronze Age**. The Bronze Age was an early period in human history. It was when people made tools from **bronze**. Bronze is a mixture of copper and tin. It's better for cutting and chopping. It was easy to shape. People became more advanced in the Bronze Age. They learned special skills. Making bronze tools was hard.

The Bronze Age ended with the Iron Age. Iron was stronger than bronze.

Some stones were taken away.

The first phase is called Stonehenge 1. Ancient people used deer antlers as shovels. They dug a big circular **ditch** and **bank**. Ditches are like holes. Banks are like walls. Ancient people made a circle monument.

The second phase is called Stonehenge 2. Ancient people built a wood building in the center. This is no longer there.

The third phase is called Stonehenge 3. Ancient people made a double ring. They **erected** bluestones in the center. Erect means to make stand. Ancient people erected sarsens in the outer circle. They kept moving the stones. Over time, Stonehenge's stones fell and broke.

# EXPLAINED BY SCIENCE

Many people still go to Stonehenge to see the summer solstice. They watch the sun rise above the Heel Stone. The Heel Stone is part of Stonehenge. Summer solstice is a day of the year. It has the longest period of daylight. It's caused by the orbit of Earth and its tilt as it goes around the sun. Summer solstice happens twice a year. It happens around June 20 for the northern half of the planet. It happens around December 20 for the southern half. After this day, the planet starts to rotate away from the sun. This means there's less daylight. The winter solstice is the day when Earth is farthest away from the sun.

Chapter Four

# ROCKY IDEAS

## What are some explanations for Stonehenge?

Stonehenge makes people wonder. There are many stories about Stonehenge.

There's the legend of the dancing giants. Giants were dancing in a circle. They turned into stones. Some people think sarsens look like giants holding hands. Stonehenge is called the "Giant's Dance."

There's an old picture of Stonehenge. A giant is shown building Stonehenge. This made people believe that giants helped build Stonehenge. Giants wanted healing stones. They went to Africa. They got big stones. They carried the stones. They brought the stones to England.

Some people believe Noah's flood wiped out the giants.

Some people think Stonehenge was made by magic. **Wizards** are men who use magic. The most powerful wizard was Merlin. Legends say that in the fifth century, there was a battle. It took place at Wiltshire. Many British soldiers were killed. They were buried in that spot. The king wanted a monument there. He wanted to honor the dead. Giants had built a henge in Ireland. The king wanted that henge. Merlin used his magic. He moved the stones. He put them in a circle. He created Stonehenge.

Historian Geoffrey of Monmouth made the Merlin story popular.

# INVESTIGATION TIPS

- Talk to someone who's been to Stonehenge. Ask about what they learned and saw. Ask how they felt.
- Study written records about Stonehenge. Do research. Read everything you can. Read books. Read articles. Go to the library.
- Study maps. Know the area.
- Study photographs. Take your own photographs.
- Bring a trowel. This is an archaeologist's most important tool. It carefully removes thin layers of soil from items.
- Take lots of notes. Every detail matters.
- Create a site grid. This is a special map. It's a precise map of everything in the area.

People think aliens also built the Pyramids in Egypt.

Some people think Stonehenge is a place of power. They think it's a **portal**. Portals are doors to another world. Stonehenge is believed to be a time machine.

Some people blame aliens. Aliens were believed to have made Stonehenge. They modeled it after the solar system. They needed a place to land their spaceships.

There's an ancient alien theory. Ancient people did amazing things. Stonehenge is an example. But ancient people didn't have advanced tools. Some people think aliens helped them. Aliens were thought to be smarter. They came to Earth thousands of years ago. They shared their knowledge. They guided humans.

Chapter Five

# BURIED BENEATH THE STONES

What is the most popular scientific explanation for Stonehenge?

Scientists don't believe in aliens, magic, or giants. They think Stonehenge was a **cemetery**. Cemeteries are places where dead bodies are buried.

Mike Parker Pearson is an **archaeologist**. Archaeologists are special scientists. They're experts. They study human history. Pearson and his team studied Stonehenge. They found over 50,000 **cremated** bone fragments. Cremated means to burn dead bodies.

Pearson thinks people were buried there before Stonehenge was built. He thinks bluestones were **gravestones**. Gravestones are markers. Pearson thinks Stonehenge is a giant circular cemetery.

Some people think Stonehenge is a temple.

# REAL-WORLD CONNECTION

Tommy Gun is an artist. He's known for large-scale sculptures. He's known for using machine parts. He wanted to celebrate the summer solstice. He made a copy of Stonehenge. He used 18 scrap cars. He stacked the cars. He put them bumper to bumper. He did this on the lawn of London's South Bank. It took Gun 3 months to do this. His work stands about 17 feet (5 m) tall. It weighs 36 tons. It can handle a strong storm. He calls his work the Skodahenge. Skoda is the name of a Czech auto company. Gun said, "It is made entirely from old car parts, which taps into my own childhood growing up on a farm where I used to love building and creating things with pieces of discarded machinery."

Pearson also found a special stick. He found a little bowl. He thinks this means there were **ceremonies**. Ceremonies are special events to honor people. This means the dead could have been leaders. He thinks only important people were buried at Stonehenge. Pearson said, "Clearly, these were special people in some way." He thinks up to 240 people were buried at Stonehenge.

Mike Pitts is another archaeologist. He thinks there are more dead bodies. He said, "I believe that there are hundreds more burials to be found across the site, which will tell us more of the story."

Real or not? It doesn't matter. The mystery of Stonehenge lives in people's imaginations.

Bodies were buried at Stonehenge over time.

## DID YOU KNOW?

- Avebury is another henge. It's 17 miles (27 kilometers) away from Stonehenge. It's older. It's larger.
- Prehistoric circles are called "piper stones." Some people think Stonehenge was built with music in mind. The shapes and sizes of the rocks make excellent acoustics. Acoustics are the sound environment. Stonehenge is like being in a concert hall.
- Some people think Stonehenge made music. Someone would hit the henge with a stone. Stonehenge would make sounds. It would call people to the area.
- Pigs were killed at Stonehenge. They were killed in December and January. Scientists think this means there were celebrations there.
- Some people think Stonehenge was an ancient team-building exercise. The area was trying to unite different people. Perhaps the leaders wanted people to work together to build Stonehenge.
- Some people think Stonehenge was an observatory. People go to observatories to look at space. Stonehenge could have been a way for ancient people to track the movements in the sky.
- Some people reported seeing a ghost hitchhiker. The ghost is a young woman. She wants a ride to Stonehenge. Drivers have reported seeing her in their cars. They're shocked. They look again. The ghost disappears.
- Archaeologists found a wild auroch at Stonehenge. Aurochs are ancient cows.

## CONSIDER THIS!

Take a Position: **There are different ideas for why Stonehenge was built. Which ideas make sense to you? Why do you think it was built? Argue your point with reasons and evidence.**

Say What? **Research "America's Stonehenge." Explain what it is. Compare it to Stonehenge. Explain how they're similar. Explain how they're different.**

Think About It! **People give tours of Stonehenge. Pretend that you're a tour guide. What would you tell people? Create a plan for a tour. Create a brochure.**

### LEARN MORE


- Aronson, Marc. *If Stones Could Speak: Unlocking the Secrets of Stonehenge*. Washington, DC: National Geographic, 2010.
- Kelley, True. *Where Is Stonehenge?* New York: Grosset and Dunlap, 2016.
- Omoth, Tyler. *Handbook to Stonehenge, the Bermuda Triangle, and Other Mysterious Locations*. North Mankato, MN: Capstone Press, 2017.

## GLOSSARY

**archaeologist** (ahr-kee-AH-luh-jist) special scientist who studies human history

**bank** (BANGK) wall

**bluestones** (BLOO-stohnz) large stones that have hints of blue when wet or freshly broken

**bronze** (BRAHNZ) material made of copper and tin

**Bronze Age** (BRAHNZ AYJ) period of early human history when people used bronze tools

**cemetery** (SEM-ih-ter-ee) place where dead bodies are buried

**ceremonies** (SER-uh-moh-neez) special events to honor people

**cremated** (KREE-mate-ed) burned dead bodies

**ditch** (DICH) hole, trench

**erected** (ih-REKT-id) to make stand tall, to build

**gravestones** (GRAVE-stohnz) markers of dead bodies

**henge** (HENJ) circle of stones or wooden posts

**hippies** (HIP-eez) people who are free spirts and don't believe in traditional values

**megaliths** (MEG-uh-lithz) single large stones arranged in a circle

**monument** (MAHN-yew-muhnt) structure that is built to honor something or someone

**portal** (POR-tuhl) door to another world

**sarsens** (SAR-sunz) really large stones

**upright** (UHP-rite) standing straight up

**wizards** (WIZ-urdz) men with magical powers

## INDEX



## ABOUT THE AUTHOR

Dr. Virginia Loh-Hagan is an author, university professor, former classroom teacher, and curriculum designer. She'd like to see Stonehenge one day. She lives in San Diego with her very tall husband and very naughty dogs.